R

School Days Around the World

"*I don't mind if I have to sit on the floor at school. All I want is education.*"

— Malala Yousafzai

School Days Around the World

Written by
Margriet Ruurs

Illustrated by
Alice Feagan

For all the teachers and learners in my life — M.R.

To Cam, for teaching me to think outside the box — A.F.

Acknowledgments

This book would not have been possible without the help of real children around the world.
Many thanks to them and to others who provided information and help:

Cook Islands: Tamatoa and family; Maureen Goodwin; Rebecca Teinakirahi at Apii Te Uki Ou
Singapore: Raphael, Nadine and family; Katie Day
China: Michael and family; Barbara Boyer; Nancy Bai; Jane Cao
Kazakhstan: Alina and family; Sapargul Mirseitova
Ethiopia: Marta Tizazu
Kenya: Mathii; Eric and Anita Walters; Ruth Kyatha
Turkey: Bilge and family; Hamdullah Uçar; Yasemin Uçar; Mehmet Uçar
Germany: Johannes and family; Catherine Donovan
Denmark: Annika and family
Venezuela: Luciano and family; Yeni Helena Sánchez de González
Honduras: Rotary International
U.S.A.: Amy, Gwen and family; Linda Marr
Canada: Shanika and family; Kathy Kiss

Special thanks to my editor, Valerie Wyatt, for her enthusiasm.

Text © 2015 Margriet Ruurs
Illustrations © 2015 Alice Feagan

Kids Can Press acknowledges the financial support of the Government of Ontario, through
the Ontario Media Development Corporation's Ontario Book Initiative; the Ontario Arts Council;
the Canada Council for the Arts; and the Government of Canada, through the CBF,
for our publishing activity.

Published in Canada by
Kids Can Press Ltd.
25 Dockside Drive
Toronto, ON M5A 0B5

Published in the U.S. by
Kids Can Press Ltd.
2250 Military Road
Tonawanda, NY 14150

www.kidscanpress.com

Edited by Valerie Wyatt
Designed by Marie Bartholomew

This book is smyth sewn casebound.
Manufactured in Shenzhen, China, in 10/2014 by C&C Offset

CM 15 0 9 8 7 6 5 4 3 2 1

Library and Archives Canada Cataloguing in Publication

Ruurs, Margriet, 1952–, author
    School days around the world / written by Margriet Ruurs ;
illustrated by Alice Feagan.

(Around the world)
ISBN 978-1-77138-047-8 (bound)

    1. School day — Juvenile literature. 2. Schools — Juvenile literature.
I. Feagan, Alice, illustrator II. Title.

LB1556.R88 2015   j371   C2014-903328-1

Kids Can Press is a *lorus*™ Entertainment company

Contents

School Days Around the World

What is a school?
Is it a building with classrooms?
Or can it be any place where children learn?

Let's take a journey
around the world
to see what school is like
for kids in different countries.

You will meet some children who live at school and others who have to walk a long way to get there. You will see schools with libraries and computers but also schools with hardly any books at all.

Schools around the world may be very different, but children everywhere like to have friends and learn new things. Perhaps they are just like you!

Schoolchildren Around the World

Meet these children and see what their schools are like.

Shanika
Canada

Amy & Gwen
U.S.A.

Ana
Honduras

Tamatoa
Cook Islands

Luciano
Venezuela

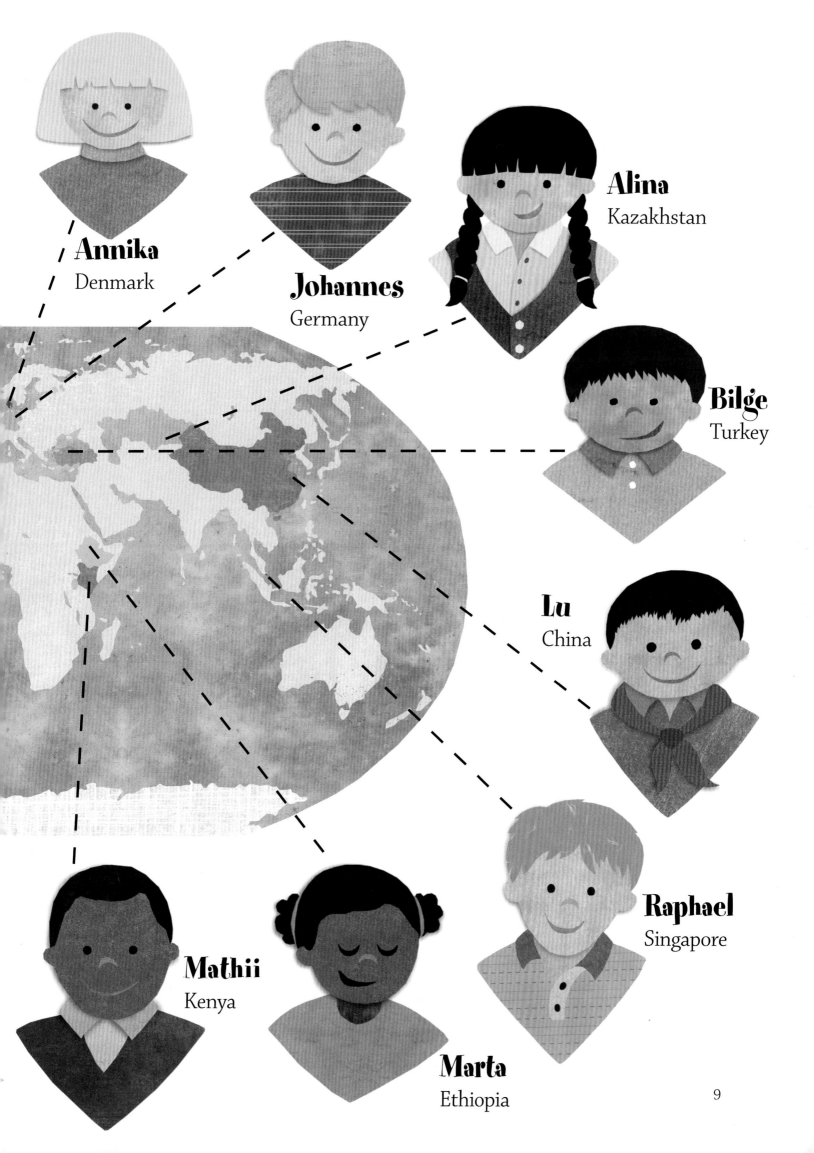

Annika
Denmark

Johannes
Germany

Alina
Kazakhstan

Bilge
Turkey

Lu
China

Mathii
Kenya

Marta
Ethiopia

Raphael
Singapore

9

Tamatoa goes to school on Rarotonga, one of the Cook Islands in the South Pacific.

Just as I slide off our family's scooter,
I hear the pounding of the wooden slit drum.
Thang-THONG-thang!
School is starting! We stream into school like a river.

I am glad that the ceiling fans are on.
It gets hot on our tropical island.
Our teacher always wears
flowers in her hair.
"*Kia orana!* Welcome!" she says.
"Let us practice the Ura language."

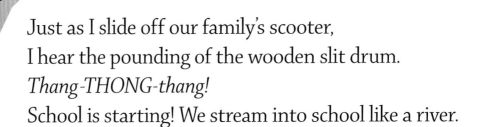

The drum sounds for lunch break.
We race to the whale-watching
fort by the sea and pretend to be
fierce warriors.

After lunch we dance *hupa*.
Swaying hips and swinging arms,
the whole school does our
traditional island dance.

11

Raphael attends an international school in Singapore.

In my class there are students
from 15 different countries.
Most of us speak several different languages.
I speak Dutch, English and Spanish.
Aaman is my best friend. He speaks Hindi,
Chinese and English.

At lunchtime we eat in the canteen.
We can choose Indian, Western or
Chinese food. My favorite is *lo mein*.

I have the best teacher in the world.
He likes taking photographs,
and so do I.
He reads to us and
helps us write stories
on the computer.

My favorite place in the whole school is the library. It has books about everything. We can take the books home, too!

Sometimes we have a craft fair to raise money to help children in other parts of the world.

Lu goes to public school in Shanghai, China.

Shanghai is a big and busy city. It takes us half an hour to drive from my home to my school.

My school is also big and busy. It has more than 2000 students! There are 43 children in my classroom. Each day we study eight different subjects, including Chinese, English, math and music. I like gym class best.

When it is time to change subjects,
there is no bell that rings.
Instead classical music plays over the intercom.
Sometimes I go to the computer lab and play games.

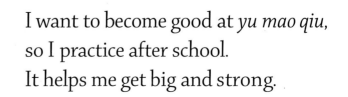

I want to become good at *yu mao qiu*,
so I practice after school.
It helps me get big and strong.

Alina goes to school in Taraz, Kazakhstan.

I am out of breath by the time I reach my classroom
on the third floor of my school. Lots of stairs!
Today it is my turn to water the plants
on the sunny windowsill.

Our teacher arrives
and we open our books.
Reading is my favorite subject.
I especially love *Kuurmash*, a
magazine for Kazakh children.

School is over at 12:30 p.m.
Grandmother is already waiting
on the big couch near the office.
"How was school?" she asks.
"It was fun," I say.
I skip rope all the way to the market.

We buy oranges, potatoes and
a bag of warm *baursaks*.
When we get home, we will
eat some with our tea.

Marta goes to school in Azezo, Ethiopia.

I walk along the dusty road to school
with my *goddegna* Ayana.
It is early morning, but already
the sun is hot on our backs.
I am blind so I hold my friend's hand tightly
as she helps me around potholes and cow patties.

There are 70 students in our
class and 500 in our school.
But many more students use the same school.
That's why I have classes only in the morning.
In the afternoon 500 more students
come to learn.

Our language is Amharic.
Someday I hope to learn English, too.
We are learning all about Ethiopia.
I listen closely to what the teacher
says as she writes it on the board.
I may not be able to see,
but I can imagine everything.

At noon Ayana and I hurry home
to help feed the ox and cow and to
fetch water from the village well.

Mathii goes to school
in Kikima, Kenya.

My friends and I live in an orphanage
because our parents died.

The sun is barely up when I hurry to school to sweep the floors.
The students and teachers arrive, and we gather at the flagpole
for *mboya* and announcements.

We learn in Kikamba, the language of our people.
We have books that were donated to our school.
I like to look at the pictures of animals and
people in different countries.
When I grow up I want to be a pilot.
Maybe then I will get to see these faraway places!

Back at the orphanage I change out of
my school uniform to do my chores.
My friends and I share meals and a room.
We do homework, talk about our day
and fall asleep when all grows quiet.

Bilge goes to school in Alatarla, Turkey.

My school is in another town.
I ride to school in an *okul taşıtı*.
Children from more than 50 villages
get to the same school in the same way.

At school we line up for the flag
ceremony, then we all go to class.
My school has a science lab
and a computer lab.
My favorite subject is math.

We all eat lunch in the big dining hall.
Then we rush outside to play soccer.

Camilla's brother Johannes lives in a boarding school in Germany.

Today is visitors' day at my big brother's school.
His school is far away from home,
so he lives there during the school year.
I like to visit him.

Part of his school is an old *schloss*.
Johannes lives in a stone house on the school grounds.
He shares a bedroom with three boys.
Students eat together with their teachers in the dining room.
Everyone has to help clear the table after meals, just like at home.

The students learn about nature and science.
They also learn how to sail.
My brother showed me a
dinghy with white sails.
I can't wait to go to school there
and learn to sail on the lake.

Johannes loves life at school. He has many friends there.
But I think he sometimes misses home a little bit —
and even me.

Annika goes to school in Copenhagen, Denmark.

My school is like two schools —
one in the city and one in the forest.
In our city school, we sit in a circle on the floor
and talk about many things.
Or we make music and sing songs.
For lunch we eat rye bread with cold meat.

Some days the school bus takes us to our forest school.
When we get there we run and climb on an old boat.
We play on swings and with a ball.

We are almost always outside, listening
to birds, learning about plants and insects.
Even in winter we are outside, bundled up
in *flyverdragter* and hats to stay warm.

Luciano goes to school in Mérida, Venezuela.

On days when I am lucky
my father drops me off at school
in the taxi he drives.

The bell rings at 8:30 a.m.
We greet our teacher.
"*Buenos días*, Professor!"
My classroom is bright green.
There are posters on the walls.
Our teacher says bright colors
help our brains learn better!

My favorite subject is music.
I play the violin and dream of
playing in a big orchestra.

School is over at 12:30 p.m.
I walk home along busy city streets.
Later I do homework and chores,
but I still have time to play soccer
with my friends.

Ana goes to school in San Luis, Honduras.

I walk an hour
from my home in the hills
to our new school.

My *padre* helped build the school.
The people from our village helped, too,
and others came from far away.
The school is made of bricks and has a metal roof.
When it rains, the water pings off
the roof. It is noisy!

30

We have two teachers who teach
us how to read and write.
I like to write stories and draw
pictures for my little brother,
who doesn't go to school yet.

Sometimes a nurse visits our school.
She teaches us how to brush our teeth and stay healthy.
One day a van comes, full of backpacks.
We each get a backpack with books and school supplies —
even running shoes!

Amy and Gwen are homeschoolers in Alaska, U.S.A.

The world is our classroom! School starts when we wake up and is over when we go to sleep. Every day is different for us. We might do math in the car, visit a tide pool or read in bed.

Our house looks like a library and
sometimes like a messy art gallery.

We go on field trips, too.
Last week we went fishing and
helped to haul in a huge halibut.
We spotted a minke whale.
Back home, we researched whales.

Even in winter we hike and camp.
Or we work by a cozy fire,
making corn husk dolls and
a First Nations longhouse from little logs.

Shanika goes to a First Nations school in Alberta, Canada.

In the morning I walk across the reserve
to school with my mom or dad.
We call it the pink school —
I guess you can see why.

First we have breakfast.
Then we do math and language arts.
We also learn our traditional Cree language.
We all have our own tablets to help us learn.

My friends and I eat lunch at school —
bannock loaded with beans and cheese.
We call them bannock tacos!

After lunch, *Kokum* Anita
sometimes comes to tell stories.
Other elders teach us powwow dances,
drumming and how to raise a teepee.
They also hold feasts where they pray for us,
and our whole community shares
tea, soup, bannock and berries.

Schools Everywhere!

Teachers and students
all over the world
make every school special!

Do you have a favorite
book or magazine that you
like to read, like Alina in Kazakhstan?
Are you learning traditional dances,
like children on the Cook Islands
and in Canada?

Or do you like to help
others, like Raphael
and his friends at their
craft fair in Singapore?

Every child has the right to an education.
Education means more than just
learning to add numbers
or spell words.

It also means learning to understand
how children in other countries live.
The whole world can be a school!

A Closer Look at Schools Around the World

The schools described in this book are all real, as are the children. They, their teachers and families helped to make this an authentic look at an ordinary school day in their part of the world. They generously shared their hopes, dreams and experiences with me.

The following activities are aimed at enriching children's reading experience. Use them as is or tailor them to fit into your daily life. Even more ideas can be found on my website: www.margrietruurs.com.

Pinpointing on the Map

Using a globe or atlas, show children where they live. Then locate each of the countries in the book.

Talking About School

Discuss which school is most like yours. In what way is it similar? In what way is it different?

Talk about a typical school day for your child or children. Do they eat breakfast or lunch at school? How many students are there in their classroom? What are their favorite subjects? How would their day be different if they were homeschooled, like Amy and Gwen in Alaska (page 32)?

Get the Details

To compile the information in this book, I interviewed children, parents and teachers from around the world. Ask children to interview a family member or friend about their schooling. Help them compile questions such as: Where did you attend school? How did you get to school? What was school like for you?

Read Closely

Here are some ideas for encouraging close reading of the illustrations and text:

- Children around the world get to school in different ways. Some have to walk a long distance (Ana in Honduras, page 30), some travel by van (Bilge in Turkey, page 22) and others live at school (Johannes in Germany, page 24). How does your child or children get to school? Ask them to draw a picture of themselves going to school.

- Children on the Cook Islands (page 10) and at the First Nations school in Canada (page 34) learn traditional dances. Do your children or students know any folk dances or folk songs from their cultural backgrounds?

- In which country do students learn to sail a boat? Which student loves to play badminton? Who plays the violin? Are your children also learning a special skill in school? Ask them to write a story about it.

Helping Others to Learn

Not all children around the world are able to go to school. Sometimes there simply is no school or teacher. Sometimes they live too far away or their families do not have money for books or uniforms. An education can help children overcome poverty and get ahead in life. Here are some ways to help other children attend school:

- Canadian author Eric Walters and his family started an organization called Creation of Hope in Kenya: www.creationofhope.com. Because of this organization, Mathii (page 20) now lives at an orphanage and attends school. You and your children can help by raising money and making a donation. For a small amount of money, you can purchase a blanket for the orphanage, a chicken or a school uniform.

- On page 30 you read about the new school in Honduras that Ana attends. It was built with the aid of Rotary

International. Find out if there is a Rotary Club in your community, and ask what they do to help children and schools and how you can be involved.

- Luciano on page 28 takes music lessons and wants to become a musician. El Sistema is a global movement that transforms the lives of children through music: www.elsistemausa.org. In Venezuela, the program teaches music to more than 300 000 of the poorest children.

There are many other organizations that build schools and libraries or fund education projects, including:

- Room to Read: www.roomtoread.org

- CODE: www.codecan.org

The students at the international school in Singapore (page 12) hold a craft fair to raise money for schools in other places. You and your children can help, too, through some simple actions:

- Collect coins or bottles to donate.

- Have a yard sale of outgrown books and toys.

- Adopt a student, a library or a school that needs help. For up-to-date contact information, email: margriet@margrietruurs.com.

Glossary

Many different writing scripts are used around the world. For example, in the Cyrillic writing script of Kazakhstan, the word *teacher* would look like this: мұғалім. In this glossary the words have been written in Latin script, which is what you are reading right now.

Pages 10–11: Cook Islands, *Ura*

akarongo (ah-kah-rong-o): listen
Kia orana (key oh-RA-nah): Welcome
tatau (tah-tow): read

Pages 12–13: Singapore, *Cantonese*

lo mein (LOH-mane): noodles

Pages 14–15: China, *Mandarin*

yu mao qiu (uuh mauw tjow): badminton

Pages 16–17: Kazakhstan, *Kazakh*

baursaks (BAUR-sahks): puffy, donut-like buns

Pages 18–19: Ethiopia, *Amharic*

goddegna (go-DECK-na): friend

Pages 20–21: Kenya, *Kikamba*

mboya (hm-BOY-ah): prayers

Pages 22–23: Turkey, *Turkish*

okul taşıtı (oh-KOOL TAH-shuh-tuh): school bus

Pages 24–25: Germany, *German*

schloss (shh-lOss): castle

Pages 26–27: Denmark, *Danish*

flyverdragter (fly-ver-DRACK-ter): snowsuits that look like flight suits

Pages 28–29: Venezuela, *Spanish*

Buenos días (BWAY-nose DEE-ahs): Good morning

Pages 30–31: Honduras, *Spanish*

padre (PAW-dray): father

Pages 34–35: Canada, *Cree*

kokum (KOH-come): grandmother